# WELLNESS AND PERSONAL DEVELOPMENT TIPS FOR THE MODERN ENTREPRENEUR

*Personal Development and Wellness Practices That Entrepreneurs Can Implement To Better Cope With Stress*

Greg Reynoso

**Greg Reynoso**

# CONTENTS

Title Page
CHAPTER 1: Personal Development     4
CHAPTER 2: Personal Development Practices and Steps     9
CHAPTER 3: How to Cope with Stress     14
About The Author     22

# INTRODUCTION

* * *

Every day a new business is opening in the growing corporate world, and the competition is becoming harder than ever. This competitive chaos can be a great deal if a person wants to start a new business on their own. Entrepreneurship is the development of a new company or the choice to work for yourself, more generally. The person who starts the new company or makes the decision on self-employment is an entrepreneur. They may be freelancers, musicians or consultants who are autonomous. Traditionally, regardless of what that company is, we think of entrepreneurs as individuals who start their businesses. The beginning of a new business can be extremely demanding due to the amount of attention and time it requires, which can cause an entrepreneur much disturbance and stress in their personal life. An entrepreneur's hectic life expects them to sacrifice life necessities such as sleep, comfort, no work, life split, stable routine, etc. Due to an entrepreneur's demanding routine, it becomes super stressful and anxious to balance the most basic aspects of their life. In order to keep the balance between personal life and business life, they will have to undertake several steps and practices for better personal development and wellness.

If you are looking for personal development practices suitable for you and want to be a better entrepreneur without it letting affect your personal life and wellness, then continue reading the following chapters of this book. The following chapters tell you how to plan for personal development and how you can remain focused on your wellbeing and growing your business skills at the same time. It also shares some strategies with you which you can implement in no time!

Have a look at each Chapter and its contents to understand better the whole concept of working under pressure and stress and how to cope with it accordingly. Due to the stressful course of entrepreneurship, we witness an ever-evolving landscape of the business world, but what remains hidden in this transformation's limelight is entrepreneurs' stressed life. Entrepreneurship is not a cakewalk; instead, it is a laboriously challenging job with its fair share of incentives and pitfalls.

# CHAPTER 1: PERSONAL DEVELOPMENT

❋ ❋ ❋

Personal development is an ongoing and life-long process in which everyone may develop their quality of life by discovering themselves, improving their own strengths and potential, and raising the chances of achieving significant goals and ambitions, basically, by focusing on our own development in our lives by concentrating on our own personal growth by setting concrete goals in this direction. Even people passionate about their business and who love to go to work can experience stress and anxiety from work. Every person experiences work stress at some point in life, so they need to formulate a personal development practice to keep themselves better and well. Personal developmental goals vary for every individual as all of us want different things from our lives. Thus, the goals can only be set by thorough thinking and acknowledging the necessary events and responsibilities in life. Personal developmental activities are of all kinds and vary for different people.

This Chapter will focus on how to prioritize your life in order to bring balance in life. It will also examine the different priorities for women and men and how to sort them out. Moreover, this

Chapter will discuss how prioritizing essentialities can help in making a plan.

### Personal Development Plan

Currently, there are approximately 582 million entrepreneurs around the world. Out of which, females round up to almost 252 million, and the rest are male entrepreneurs. Female entrepreneurs tend to have more hectic and stressful routines than males. They ought to have an outdoing plan than males. However, it does not mean that the male entrepreneurs do not experience stress and anxiety. Many analysts say that males find it very hard to tell themselves when to take a break from work. Reportedly, they work tirelessly for the betterment of their business. Every entrepreneur goes through the same level of stress when it comes to their business. They prefer sacrificing their lives over the business, which causes a huge amount of disturbance.

In addition to this, employed life is more manageable than the entrepreneur life. Job life is limited; one always knows when to stop and what exactly their job requires them to work. The ease comes from the limited amount of work with a promised price while entrepreneurship is risk dependent work, every step can make or break the deal step. How important work is to their identity is one interesting thing about entrepreneurs. The work satisfaction of entrepreneurs is more closely linked to their satisfaction with their lives, families, and themselves, relative to full-time workers. In other words, in all facets of their life, they are likely to be unhappy if they are dissatisfied with their business venture. Moreover, the entrepreneurs try to focus on every detail about their business, from work sketch to work completion. Unlike a job, entrepreneurs need to think about the decisions they will make. The cost-benefit analysis and out-of-the-box thinking for profit maximization can be a very daunting experience. Hence, personal development and wellness measures are necessary for entrepreneurs to deal with hecticness and stressful life.

Being an entrepreneur, it is hard not to be an all-rounder. Every entrepreneur is an all-rounder in various ways, yet, they find it hard to prioritize the important events in their personal life. The amount of sacrifice their personal life gives for the business is beyond comprehension. The most important step to personal development is prioritization, which will help seduce weekly tasks. In order to make a weekly plan, first, the acknowledgment of necessary tasks is essential. For example, if you have a big meeting and a wedding to attend in the coming week, get done with the meeting at the earliest day of the week so you have time for the wedding later in the week. To say, get the hardest work project done as early of the week as possible so as the week proceeds on you will require less energy at work and more time to focus on the off-work things.

### Concentration on Priorities

During work do not take responsibility for everything. Train your team and trust your team enough to rely on them for certain work. An individual cannot work after a certain limit. There have to be other ways to get the work done without taking all the responsibility and stress on yourself. The suggestion is that you focus only on the matters that will drive growth and development, you would be surprised to realize how much time is wasted throughout the day. Pay attention to the projects that will help you improve your skills in a better efficient way and get the work which you have already done and know from your team. Even though people keep telling you that it is your business and that you will need to do the work. It is not your duty to keep doing all the work. Do not listen to them and do not tire and exhaust yourself! Just focus on the main projects and then focus on your personal life and health.

In addition to this, it is alright to drop the perfectionist trait. It is understandable that you have worked tirelessly to build this business and that now you want everything according to your plan and exactly the way you wanted things to be. As people say every company looks messy on the inside, so do not get stressed if you do not see a thing happening the way you desired it. However, you have to take the risk of letting things be the way they are. This may be hard at first but with practice, you can master this technique. You have heard or read all the quotes like without hard work you cannot achieve anything. However, it is not always the case, in fact, sometimes smart work can outwork the hard work. So, keep learning and practicing the art of smart work over hard work. Moving forward, it is reported that male and female entrepreneurs have a lot to differ mostly in the routines. They have different duties and roles to play in society along with different attributes. For example, unlike men, women generally are burdened with household duties as well. They need to take care of the family and keep the house in running order. This is why the number of female entrepreneurs is lesser than male entrepreneurs. Contrary to this, the female can have a sustainable career and life as well only if they prioritize work and life, and also by limiting the working time. Males can schedule their week ahead of their time to organize and prioritize the important tasks of the week. Whereas women would need to decide on what will require the most time in the upcoming week.

To state, do not take the stress of prioritization, because the pressure of running a business never goes away. Being an entrepreneur, you will always find something is lit on fire but in reality, you just have to focus on the bigger stuff rather than noticing every detail. Let your team help you with your stress and let them deal with things that bother you. These strategies of prioritizing the important tasks a week ahead can prove to be an amazing tool for getting the harder and bigger tasks at the earliest. It will also help in dividing the burden of projects on the days when you can devote time and when you cannot spare time for work. There are greater chances of getting the most productivity out of this technique as it will make headway on the goals that really matter to you and your work. Overall, it is an alive and running business so, every day brings a new challenge and requirement. It will always look messier from the inside and if it does look good then it is a big red flag that you are dealing with matters that are urgent and not the matters that essential. Rather than focusing on what is urgent and seems easy to get done. First, pay attention to the important and hard to get done projects. You can also become a better leader with the help of personal development, which will help reduce staff turnover. You will develop the capacity to instill trust in all members of the team, who will start to follow your lead.

# CHAPTER 2: PERSONAL DEVELOPMENT PRACTICES AND STEPS

✻ ✻ ✻

In achieving your business goals, becoming a good entrepreneur requires hard work and consistency. Interestingly, wellbeing has a huge influence on how persistent an entrepreneur is in pursuit of these objectives. Low-welfare and high-exhaustion entrepreneurs are less inspired to continue their new business plan. You know that outcomes and success take time if you are an entrepreneur. Before giving the organization a fair chance, leaving means you've wasted your time, energy, and resources. Working on your personal wellbeing will motivate you to get through the hard times and continue to chase those dreams! For a cause, you started this venture - don't let fatigue and tirelessness derail you! This Chapter inculcates the discussions about the personal development practices that entrepreneurs bring in their lives for the betterment and wellbeing of their health and business.

There are several areas where personal development can take

place but these five are the most common areas.

- Mental Development
- Social development.
- Spiritual Development
- Emotional Development
- Physical Development

**Mental Development**

The First and the foremost improvement and growth of your mind. You may engage in many personal development programs for mental development. To develop your skills, some examples are taking a class, reading a book, or watching an interesting YouTube video. You will see progress in your career, improved productivity, and so much more by setting aside some time each day, or each week. Anxiety and depression can shut you away from the world and yourself due to immense entrepreneurial pressure. Entrepreneurship in your life brings ambition and obsession. Unfortunately, at the detriment of relationships and wellbeing, you may often experience a compulsive desire to get things moving. There is an increased risk of depression as a result and, thus, of falling into addiction. This is a turning point that is not understood by many entrepreneurs and they develop an opioid addiction, painkiller addiction, alcohol addiction, etc. You have to recognize the causes that make you nervous and anxious to prevent all of this. You need to be careful of the early signs of possible mental health problems such as friend isolation, altered sleeping and eating patterns, apathy, and more. Seek medical advice if necessary, because there is no shame in seeking treatment and having someone to speak to. In the corporate sector environment, mental health concerns are still a pressing issue that must be tackled. In reality, more and more individuals are becoming entrepreneurs and it is in the interest of everyone that their mental wellbeing should be handled. Remember, It is the pursuit of personal development to enhance the quality of life and to achieve one's dreams and aspirations. So, if your mind is tired how can you expect it works completely. Rest, Reset and Restart!

## Social Development

The second category is all about making communication easier. This group is the most ignored, in my view. Social personal development, however, is an important activity to practice. We, humans, are social animals, who require the human connection to survive. Take out time to meet the friends and family. Take out time to go on events and meet new people. This will enhance the communicative and confidence skills. This is where a strong support net, in the form of your friends, family, and colleagues, plays a crucial role in your life. On social connectivity, expanding networks, and encouraging interactions, a competitive business world runs. In fact, no entrepreneur has ever succeeded without an efficient network and support system in the past. So, it can be inward, outward, or a combination of the two; You need to reach out to them, fix the problems easily, and move forward. Mentors are fantastic and assistance is at the door by getting one on your support team. Both things that can assist with personal social growth are learning a foreign language, improving your public speaking skills, and committing to doing more active listening.

## Spiritual Development

Moreover, for each entity, spiritual personal growth may mean something distinct. Something that gives you comfort and helps you relate to your true self is the best way that I know how to explain it. From spending time in prayer and reading your Bible to taking a nature walk or meditation, the things that come under this category may be everything. I would suggest to engage in a Bible study or interact with people from the church during the spiritual personal growth period. Discussing the message on Sunday from the sermon may fill up the cup unlike anything else would.

## Personal Development

The fourth category of personal development is, personal emotional development can, well, be emotional. Because of this, brushing it off can be easy. I did my share of doing that. It wasn't good behavior, I realized. The truth is that holding back and shaking off your feelings just makes things harder when they eventually come out. Some examples of how you can deal with it are here include journaling, mood monitoring, talking sessions with a friend or family member, or even a counselor for that matter.

## Physical Development

Moving forward, we made it through the last of our five groups. You can see by now that personal growth, rightly practiced, is all about the whole self. When it comes time to select your personal development operations, it will be important to remember. Personal physical growth is about a lot more than exercise. To get the full picture of this group, you'll also want to include eating and sleeping habits, to name a few. Some examples of operations include working out, having 7-9 hours of sleep each night, prepping meals, and going to the doctor's office for routine checkups. You will be on the way to being your best physical self by developing better habits around exercise, healthy eating, and sleep. Find out what activity is pleasurable for you by trying out new activities.

Finally, it can be said that there is not much room for entrepreneurs to play with due to the shortage of time. However, there are still many things that can contribute to the personal development process of entrepreneurs. As Abraham Lincoln once said: "Give me six hours to chop down a tree and I will spend the first four sharpening the axe". Every entrepreneur needs to sharpen their axe first to increase productivity and save time. If entrepreneurs master these areas of personal development then their life would become much easier and organized. Due to the planning and sketching, everyone can sort out their hectic and stressful life. The more you learn, the better job you provide, and the greater the reward you get. Plus, it helps you stay motivated by personal development, making you aware that there is always something to enhance and that can make a huge difference. It will also help you feel happy and satisfied, understanding that you are evolving and adapting as necessary.

# CHAPTER 3: HOW TO COPE WITH STRESS

✽ ✽ ✽

**Kind of stress that entrepreneurs face**

Stress comes from many places, both inside your business and beyond the walls of the office. Stress can leak into the other from one source. Too many entrepreneurs bring home with them their business stress, which has a bad impact on their marriage, kids, and overall quality of life. Similarly, the incorporation of family and social stress into the workplace creates challenges to doing good work and achieving your goals. Businesses present more than enough possible stress points on their own.

A leader can be defocused by partners, cofounders, board members, investors, clients, suppliers, rivals, government agencies, and macroeconomic fluctuations. The bad news is that none of these stressors can be avoided-they are going to track you down. The way you handle stress defines how well you and your organization perform.

**Traits to cope with stress**

Many stress-related issues come from humans and their behavior and not from mechanics! There should always be a positive attitude towards the workplace and employees. One should always go for the traits that help with the work stress and not cause it.

- One of the traits is being optimized, entrepreneurs are optimists. Pay attention, stay optimistic, and realize that the chances of success remain high by being clever and constructive.
- Secondly, courage is the quality of mind that enables you to face difficulty without fear. Fear commonly comes from the unknown, and you are a learning machine. Banish the unknown and you become fearless.
- Thirdly, it makes them at ease to truly interact with individuals and helps you to consider their wants, interests, and desires. Through your people, you succeed, so know them.
- Fourth, keeping cash available is another good thing to avoid stress. There was no company failing to have so much cash on hand. Manage capital, prevent debt, and be frugal. This removes the most lethal start-up dysfunction, the endless search for capital.
- The fifth and the most important thing that can help in the reduction of stress in life can be hiring good employees. Hire people like you would select a partner. Employment is and should be viewed as such, a long-term partnership. This point brings us to the main matter that is to have good customers. Your clients and your markets can be selected by you at times. It is easier to serve a smaller group of clients very well and make them insanely happy than to badly serve and similarly annoy a lot of unrelated clients.
- Moving forward, being careful about vigilance can also help in preventing work stress. This includes closely monitoring everything and early risk identification. This is not paranoia; it's being mindful that things are changing and you need to be conscious of these changes.
- Last but the most essential point is being passionate, persistent, and determined. Don't give up ever. The moment you accept the chance to give in, so uncertainty wins. Optimism starts with the idea that you are not going to leave.
- Don't forget to give yourself time in the busy and hectic

routine of your entrepreneurial journey. Just do something every day, away from all of those professional tasks, that make you happy. It will help you cope with stress and anxiety, for sure. Spend a few minutes creating something new, loving the process instead of the outcome, and, most importantly, making mistakes.
- Since a work-life balance is very essential to keep mental health problems at bay, it is as important for you to invest in yourself as in your company. Exercise and balanced eating are both effective ways to take care of your mental health.
- Interesting practices such as open water swimming, jogging, or practicing yoga and meditation can be included. Connecting with nature will give you a calming and peaceful impact as well.
- Two of the main contributors to work-related stress are unpredictability and deadlines. These two variables may play a crucial role because the achievement depends primarily on how they can be treated and addressed properly. In general terms, the workload of an entrepreneur falls into two groups - physical and psychological.

**Take Care of Your Health**

By developing a stable mental foundation and gaining insight on how to prioritize your activities, you need to handle all of them. In your everyday life, you will increasingly find an endless workload, such as managing staff, preparing for the future of the company, and attending multiple meetings. The value of working smarter, instead of harder, should therefore also be known. You need to prioritize various goals and assign minor tasks for each goal and establish a time structure for each of them in order to handle them well. Ultimately, based on your talents and experiences, settle on the activities that can be accomplished efficiently by other people. Running a start-up company requires a lot of responsibilities, transparency, and mental endurance without a single shred of doubt. The amount of tension you experience and the weight of inherent ambiguity can often become intolerable for you. You have to build and retain mental toughness in order to thrive, which will keep your emotions and self-talk optimistic and you will be able to resist behaviors that lead to negativity. You have to be emotionally secure to be a competent leader so that you make good decisions under pressure. Even when nothing is really in your favor, a greater mental resilience helps you stay put. To get ready for a change, you need to inculcate flexibility and adaptability. In the face of continuous pressures, you should develop a calm demeanor so that you can deal with stressful situations effectively.

Additionally, Deprivation of sleep, poor nutrition, overwork, and lack of physical activity are all factors that can perpetuate the response to stress and ultimately generate disease or illness. Therefore, while it is better than nothing to indulge in only one aspect of healthy living (such as a healthy diet), disease prevention involves a commitment to the body and mind of the whole person. While it can be difficult for some to change, apply the same core principles to your health as you would to your company and structure your' plan for a healthier you' as you would a business plan: identify your intent, set goals and set a clear path to achieve success, and ask for help from a healthcare professional if you need some assistance.

**Benefits of Personal Development**

Moreover, there are several benefits of taking care of one's own health by inculcating personal developmental practices in life. One benefit is that there are a number of promising opportunities for growth and development. Entrepreneurs need to be able to identify the correct opportunities for a new company to expand. Where others don't, they see opportunities. Interestingly, research suggests that successful business opportunities are more likely to be noticed by safe entrepreneurs, whereas entrepreneurs with decreased wellbeing can also miss those opportunities. Studies clearly indicate that well being is central to being a good entrepreneur. In fact, some entrepreneurs think that getting high well being is a sign of their success. Make sure you take the time to nurture your wellbeing whether you intend to start your own company or have already ventured out on your own. Don't let yourself get too burned out, tired, or sad. This will affect your ability to achieve your goals, find excellent opportunities, and create a high-performing company!

Similarly, another benefit is that it will enhance the business performance Obviously, entrepreneurs want to create successful companies, and the success of those companies depends on their founders' wellbeing! Research shows, overall, that happier entrepreneurs have higher-performing companies. Also, the opposite has been found. They are more likely to face financial difficulties with their new venture if anyone is generally dissatisfied. Being happy as an entrepreneur makes the venture more profitable, similar to the 'happy, productive worker' concept. Creating your own company can be thrilling and rewarding, but in all facets of your life, make sure you reflect on your happiness. You may have no spare time for yourself, friends, family, and hobbies, but don't neglect them entirely! Keep the faith in your relationships and take time to do those things that you love.

The hard to ignore the beneficial factor of personal development practices is you become a very self-aware human being. Nothing is a motivator more powerful than the knowledge of oneself. Knowing your strengths and when to request assistance saves time and reduces stress. When you take on everyday tasks, the effect is better quality work and more trust. You can be motivated by a personal growth plan to be more self-aware and to increase your leadership capabilities. It will also assist you in work to resolve and transform strengths from weaknesses. This can allow the entrepreneurs to evaluate their own personalities and weaknesses which will help them know about the area where the development is needed. Perhaps it's time to consider how you can incorporate personal development into your company if you are feeling listless or overwhelmed. You will be able to reduce stress, increase productivity, and find a better overall work/life balance by concentrating on areas that allow you to better master how you approach work.

## Conclusion

A personal development plan is a method used by entrepreneurs to concentrate their resources on areas of personal growth. Think of this eBook as a guide to your professional life and there have been created a few simple tips to follow to help you out. A lot of people follow contemporary successful entrepreneurs for inspiration and motivation, and rightfully so. They make public speeches and attract eager listeners, write books and articles on motivation, and tell their stories of success. While all this seems to be an ideal lifestyle and a state of fulfillment, a price has to be paid even by entrepreneurs. Generating wealth isn't the only indicator of business performance. As a company owner, to truly enjoy the entrepreneurial journey, it is vital that you find a work/life balance, preserve your health and continue to grow. Out of many, one way is to create or follow a personal development plan to help with the stress and hecticness of running a business. Paying attention to a personal development strategy in a company has a lot of up-side. It can lead to you becoming a stronger business owner with a healthier business outlook and personal wellness as well. Expanding your skills, learning new things, and working on yourself will help you in your personal and business life, more than you can imagine, and it will encourage you to take risks with more confidence. You will, however, begin to learn how to take calculated risks that will not be detrimental to your business. Instead, because of the tremendous amount of trust and skills you have developed through your personal growth journey, you can concentrate on your progress with little or no obstacles!

# ABOUT THE AUTHOR

**Greg Reynoso**

Greg Reynoso is an American Writer, Producer and Entrepreneur who is best known for his role in starting Linq Magazine, an online magazine showcasing the best independent music artists and rising brands.

www.ingramcontent.com/pod-product-compliance
Lightning Source LLC
Chambersburg PA
CBHW031526210526
45464CB00007B/3028